44

Stars and Constellations

By Gregory Vogt

Steadwell
Books

Raintree Steck-Vaughn Publishers

A Harcourt Company

Austin · New York
www.steck-vaughn.com

OUR UNIVERSE

Published by Raintree Steck-Vaughn Publishers,
an imprint of Steck-Vaughn Company.

Library of Congress Cataloging-in-Publication Data
Vogt, Gregory.
    Stars and constellations/by Gregory Vogt.
        p.cm.--(Our universe)
    Includes index.
    ISBN 0-7398-3115-1
    1. Stars--Juvenile literature. 2. Constellations--Juvenile literature.
[1. Stars. 2. Constellations.] I. Title.
QB801.7.V64 2000
523.8--dc21

00-041313

Printed in the United States of America
10 9 8 7 6 5 4 3 2 1 W 02 01 00

Produced by Compass Books

Photo Acknowledgments
Don Figer (STScI) and NASA, title page, 14, 20, 32; NASA, 6; Solar &
Heliospheric Observatory (SOHO). SOHO is a project of international
cooperation between ESA and NASA, 9, 10, 11; Hubble Heritage Team
(AURA/STScI/NASA), cover, 16, 22, 35; C. R. O'Dell (Rice University) and
NASA, 18; Roeland P. van der Marel (STScI), Frank C. van den Bosch
(University of Washington), and NASA, 24; H. Bond (STScI) and NASA, 26; L.
Walter (State University of New York at Stony Brook) and NASA, 28; NASA, 36;
Roger Ressmeyer/Corbis, 38; A. Dupree (CfA), NASA, ESA, 42

Content Consultant
David Jewitt
Professor of Astronomy
University of Hawaii Institute for Astronomy

Contents

Diagram of a Star

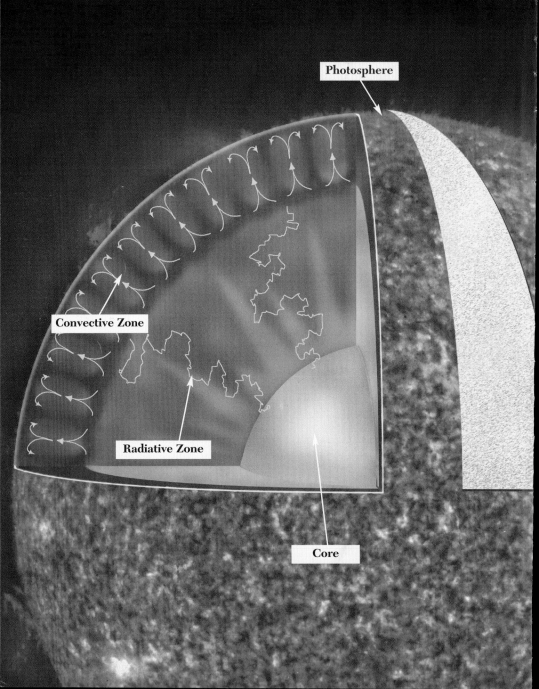

Photosphere

Convective Zone

Radiative Zone

Core

A Quick Look at Stars

What are stars?
A star is a ball of very hot gases. Stars turn their hydrogen gas into helium and energy. The energy is given off as heat and light.

Where do stars come from?
Stars are born and stars die in huge gas and dust clouds called nebulas.

What do stars look like?
Stars can be different colors and sizes. They can be white, yellow, red, or blue. A star's color depends on how hot it is. Huge stars are called giant stars. Small stars are called dwarf stars.

What are constellations?
A constellation is a group of stars that forms a pattern in the sky when seen from Earth.

How many constellations are there?
There are 88 constellations.

How do constellations get their names?
People named constellations after things the star patterns looked like, such as people or animals.

Light from thousands of stars shines on Earth. This white stream of stars is the Milky Way.

About Stars

The black night sky is full of little white dots of light. These are stars. Stars are giant balls of hot gases that give off light and heat. The stars in the sky look small and dim because they are very far away from Earth. They would look huge and bright if they were close to Earth.

Astronomers are scientists who study objects in space. They believe there are billions of stars in our universe. Astronomers study stars to find out what gases make up stars. They try to learn how stars form and how stars die.

Stars are hard to see because they are so far away. So astronomers use telescopes to get a closer look at them. A telescope makes faraway objects appear clearer and closer.

Parts of Stars

Some stars are too far away for astronomers to study in depth. They must study stars close to Earth to learn about stars. The closest star to Earth is the Sun. Astronomers study the Sun to find out about the structure of stars. They have learned that the Sun and other stars are made up of layers of gases.

The center of a star is the core. The core is the hottest part of a star. The gravity and mass from outer layers of gas creates pressure on the gas in the core. Gravity is a force that attracts objects to each other. Mass is the amount of matter an object contains. Matter is anything that has weight and takes up space. The pressure caused by gravity and mass crushes the gas into a tight, heavy ball.

A layer of slightly cooler gases called the radiative zone surrounds the core. This is the thickest layer of a star. Energy from the core bounces around the radiative zone. It can take more than one million years for energy to travel through the radiative zone.

The convective layer is a thin layer around the radiative zone. This layer has large cells of moving gases. The cells boil upward to the star's surface. These cells carry gases and energy to the surface of the star.

The surface of a star is an active place. Hot gas
bubbles rise to the star's surface. Explosions on the
surface send fiery gas streams shooting into space.
The surface also sends most of the star's light and
heat into space.

An atmosphere surrounds the surface of a star. An
atmosphere is a layer of gases that surrounds an
object in space. The atmosphere of the Sun and other
stars can stretch out for millions of miles into space.

Atoms

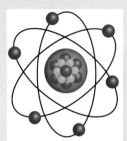

Atoms are the tiniest part of matter. An atom is made of three kinds of particles. They are protons, neutrons, and electrons. In an atom's center is a nucleus. Protons and neutrons are inside the nucleus. Electrons orbit around the nucleus.

People need light and heat from the Sun to survive on Earth.

Making Starlight and Heat

Stars are mainly made of hydrogen gas and helium gas. Temperatures in the core of a star are greater than at the star's surface. The outer layers of gas are very heavy. Their gravity pulls on the core, and the core's gravity pulls on the layers. The gravity and mass of the outer layers create pressure on the gas inside the core. This makes the gas thick and hot.

A special process begins when temperatures in a star's core reach 18 million° Fahrenheit (10 million° C). The heat and pressure of the outer gas layers squeeze hydrogen atoms inside the core together. The hydrogen atoms join together and make a new atom. The new atom is helium. This process is called fusion.

A star uses only some of its hydrogen to make helium. During fusion, leftover matter is changed into energy. The energy flows from the core to the surface of the star. The star's surface releases this energy into space as waves of light and heat.

Fusion is always happening in the core of a living star. It continues to happen in stars until they die.

This special picture of the Sun shows its energy flowing into space.

A Long Journey

The starlight astronomers see from Earth is very old. After a star's core releases energy, the energy must travel through the radiative and convective zones to the surface of the star. The energy follows a slow outward path through the radiative zone. The energy bounces and zigzags like a ball in a pinball machine. After about one million years, the energy finally reaches the star's surface.

Once on the surface, the energy flashes away from the star as light. Starlight travels outward in all directions. It moves into space at a speed of 186,000 miles (300,000 km) per second.

Rays of light spread apart as they move outward from a star into space. The light is very bright when it is close to the star. The light dims as it gets farther away from the star.

The Sun is millions of miles away from Earth. But light travels so fast that sunlight released from the Sun's surface reaches Earth in just eight minutes. Other stars are billions of miles away from Earth. It takes millions of years for light from distant stars to travel through space and reach Earth.

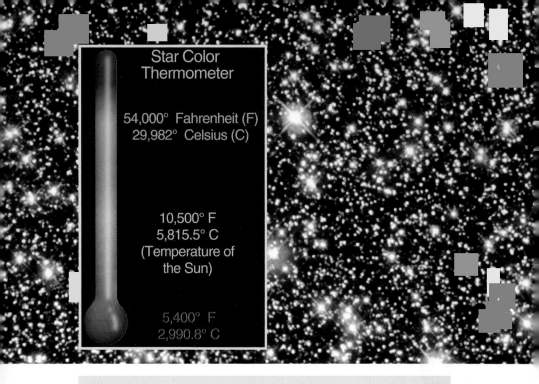

Star Color Thermometer

54,000° Fahrenheit (F)
29,982° Celsius (C)

10,500° F
5,815.5° C
(Temperature of
the Sun)

5,400° F
2,990.8° C

> **Stars are different colors, depending on how hot they are.**

Star Color

Stars can be several colors. A star's color depends on how hot it is. Very hot stars are blue. Blue stars reach temperatures of more than 54,000° Fahrenheit (30,000° C). Stars with medium temperatures are yellow or white. Cool stars are red. Red stars are less than 5,400° Fahrenheit (3,000° C).

The Sun is a yellow star. The temperature at its surface is about 10,000° Fahrenheit (5,700° C). It is about 80 times hotter than the hottest desert on Earth.

Star Brightness

Astronomers measure a star's brightness. A star's brightness can show astronomers how large and hot the star is. Brightness also helps astronomers tell how far the star is from Earth. Dimmer stars are usually farther away from our planet.

Astronomers use two terms to describe a star's brightness. The apparent brightness is how bright a star looks from Earth. From Earth, a distant bright supergiant star may look dimmer than a smaller, faint star that is close to Earth. A star's absolute brightness measures how bright a star really is. The absolute brightness of a supergiant star would be greater than that of a small, dim star.

Star brightness is hard to measure. The brightness people see from Earth depends on how far away a star is. It also depends on how hot it is. The amount of dust between a star and Earth can affect how bright it looks, too. The dust will block some of the star's light from reaching Earth.

The size of a star also affects its brightness. Stars can be different sizes. They can be small dwarfs, medium-sized stars, or giant stars. Giant-sized stars give off more light than smaller stars. This makes them much brighter even than smaller, hotter stars.

Hundreds of stars are forming in this nebula in Galaxy NGC 4214.

Life Cycle of a Star

The space between stars, planets, and other objects in outer space is not empty. It contains small amounts of gas and dust that people cannot see.

In some places, gravity pulls the dust and gas into clouds. The thick clouds of dust and gas are called nebulas. Stars are born in nebulas. They also die in nebulas.

The dust in nebulas is made up of tiny, solid particles. The particles are mainly made of carbon and silicates. They may be made up of rocky materials. Dust grains may also be coated in ice.

Stars are made of gases that come from nebulas. Hydrogen is the main gas in nebulas. Nebulas may also contain helium, oxygen, and nitrogen gases.

Protostars

Stars are not living creatures. But astronomers describe stars as having life cycles. A star's life cycle includes birth, life, and death.

A star's life cycle begins inside a nebula. Many stars can be born inside one nebula. Gravity pulls some of the nebula's particles of gas and dust together. Thick clumps of gas and dust form. Each clump has a gravitational pull. This pulls the clumps toward each other. They begin to rotate and orbit.

Over millions of years, the clumps grow. The gas and dust in the center of each clump get hotter and thicker. Some of the clumps are likely to become stars. These clumps are called protostars. A protostar is very hot, but does not give off starlight or heat.

Eventually, the temperature in the protostar gets hot enough to cause fusion in its center. Fusion begins to turn hydrogen into helium and releases energy. The protostar is then a true star because it gives off light and heat.

This is a picture of the Great Orion Nebula. Many protostars are forming inside this nebula.

Most of the stars in this star cluster are middle-aged or older.

Middle Age

A middle-aged star is in the middle of its life cycle. It can stay the same for millions of years. Fusion takes place in its core continuously. The star makes helium and releases energy as heat and light.

The Sun is a middle-aged star. Scientists believe it has been turning hydrogen into helium and energy for about five billion years.

During fusion, the Sun burns up the gas it is made of. Every second, about 660 million tons (600 million metric tons) of hydrogen changes to helium in the Sun's core. This process turns 4.8 million tons (4.4 million metric tons) of hydrogen into energy. That means the Sun uses up 4.8 million tons (4.4 million metric tons) of fuel every second.

People should not worry about the Sun running out of hydrogen gas. The Sun is very large. Scientists believe it will shine for at least five billion years longer or more.

A dying star made this Ring Nebula. The star shed several of its gas layers into space.

Death

Eventually, stars use up all their fuel and die. How long this takes depends on the star. Large, hot stars use up their fuel quickly. They are the brightest stars, but they last only about 10 million years. Smaller, cooler stars like the Sun use their fuel slowly. These stars last around 10 billion years.

Star Stuff

Star explosions make new elements, such as the metals iron and nickel. Explosions toss these elements out into space. In time, the elements become part of nebulas where new stars are born. Some of the leftover gas and dust from these exploding stars will form planets. Some scientists believe Earth was formed from elements created by ancient star explosions.

Stars can die in two ways. Small, cool stars die slowly by shedding some of their gases. The outer gas layers shoot out into space. The stars become very bright and large as they shed their outer layers.

Only a small core of gases is left after the star's outer layers are gone. This core is called a white dwarf star. Over time, the white dwarf star cools and becomes a black dwarf star.

Large, hot stars die differently. They do not shed rings of gas when they die. Instead, they explode all at once. The explosion destroys the entire star. While they are exploding, stars are called supernovas. Gas and dust from supernovas sometimes form new nebulas.

The Hubble Space Telescope took this picture of dust falling into a black hole in Galaxy NGC 7052.

Black Holes

Some scientists believe that massive supergiant stars make black holes when they die. A black hole is an object in space with such great gravity that nothing moves fast enough to escape from it, not even light.

Some supergiants cave in on themselves when they die. Their outer layers fall into the core instead of exploding into space. The star gets smaller and smaller until it seems to disappear. It has then become a black hole.

But the black hole has not disappeared. It is really there, but no one can see it. It looks black because no light can leave the surface of a black hole. A black hole's gravity is too strong, and light cannot escape.

To understand this, think about jumping off Earth. A person would have to jump upward at 25,000 miles per hour (40,000 km per hour) to escape Earth's gravity field and float into space. Earth's gravity would pull a person's body back down if he or she jumped any slower.

The gravity of a black hole is much stronger than Earth's gravity. Anything coming near a black hole is pulled in and crushed. Dust and gas falling in a black hole swirl around it like water going down a drain. The swirling gas forms a disk surrounding the black hole. The disk is called an accretion disk. Astronomers look for accretion disks to find black holes.

Powerful space telescopes are needed to see white dwarf stars (inside circles) as far away as these.

Kinds of Stars

There are different kinds of stars. They have different masses, sizes, and colors.

Very small stars are called dwarfs. They are usually old stars that are running out of fuel. The diameter of a dwarf star is around 32,000 miles (53,000 km). Diameter is the distance across the center of a circle.

There are white, black, and brown dwarf stars. White dwarfs are made when sunlike stars collapse. They are are very hot. White dwarfs are very heavy for their sizes because their gases have been pressed into a very small space. On Earth, a spoonful of a white dwarf would weigh as much as a car.

> ▲ This neutron star is very hot and bright. It is only about 17 miles (28 km) across.

Black Dwarfs and Brown Dwarfs

After thousands of years, white dwarfs turn into black dwarfs. White stars run out of hydrogen gas. They cool off. When they cool, they stop giving off light. They are then called black dwarfs.

Brown dwarfs are another kind of dwarf star. Brown dwarfs are not true stars. Their cores never get hot enough to start fusion. They never give off light.

Neutron Stars

Strange things can happen to old stars. Stars 10 to 100 times more massive than the Sun can become neutron stars when they die.

Neutron stars are the smallest stars. They are only around 19 miles (30 km) in diameter. Unlike other stars, neutron stars are dark. They give off energy as radio waves instead of visible light. A radio wave is a kind of energy that travels through space.

Neutron stars are made up mostly of neutrons. These tiny particles are part of the nucleus of an atom. Gravity makes the star shrink. It changes the atoms inside the star. The star's collapse pushes the electrons into the nuclei of the atoms. The protons and electrons join together to make more neutrons.

Neutron stars are very dense, or thick. Density is the amount of matter squeezed into a given space. Matter is anything that has weight and takes up space. Objects with greater density have a great deal of matter squeezed into a small space. Neutron stars are one million times denser than white dwarf stars. One teaspoon of a neutron star weighs 440 million tons (400 million metric tons).

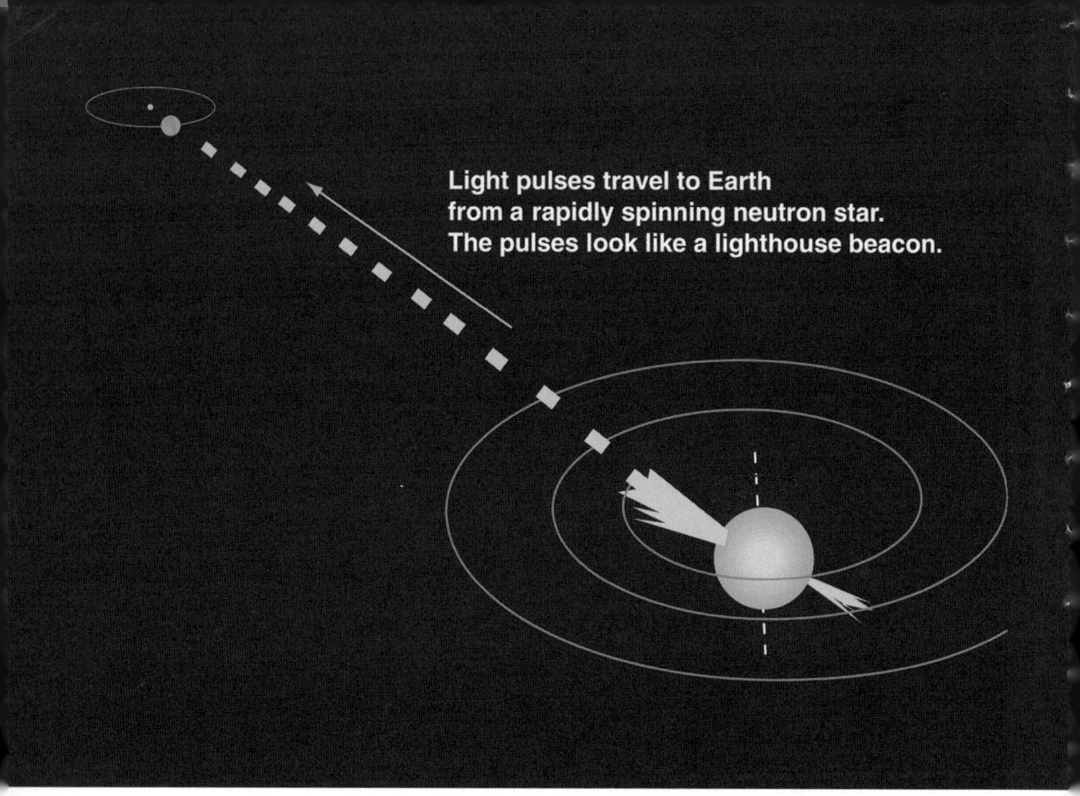

Light pulses travel to Earth from a rapidly spinning neutron star. The pulses look like a lighthouse beacon.

This diagram shows how radio waves from pulsars travel to Earth.

Pulsars

Pulsars are spinning neutron stars. They give off energy as radio waves instead of visible light.

All stars spin. Smaller stars spin faster than larger stars. Pulsars spin very fast because they are the smallest stars. Each time a pulsar spins, it releases a radio wave of energy that flows past Earth. The pulsar's spin makes radio waves spiral outward.

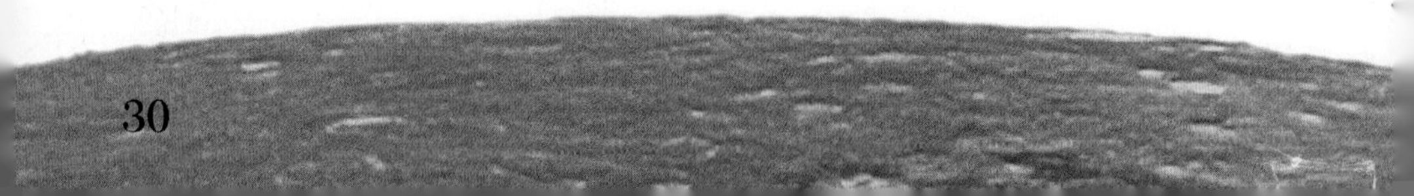

Astronomers built special radio telescopes that collect and focus radio waves. These telescopes feed radio signals into computers. The computers turn the signals into pictures.

Astronomers first discovered pulsars when they heard pulsars' radio flashes. At first, some astronomers thought the radio signals were messages from creatures in space. Later, they learned that pulsars were sending the radio signals.

British astronomer Jocelyn Bell discovered the first pulsar in 1967. She heard an object in space that released a radio wave every 1.33 seconds. This object was a pulsar. It was the first neutron star ever found.

Since 1967, astronomers have discovered hundreds of pulsars. Some pulsars spin several times in one second. Other pulsars spin hundreds of times per second.

Star Giants

Some stars are giants. They average about 602 million miles (1 billion km) in diameter. They are usually about 20 to 100 times bigger than the Sun. They are also about 100 to 1,000 times brighter than the Sun.

Some giant stars are red. The red color means they are relatively cool. Red giant stars have a surface temperature of about 5,000° Fahrenheit (2,700° C).

Other giant stars are blue. These giant stars are much hotter than red giants. But blue giants are smaller than red giants. They are up to 20 times larger than the Sun.

Blue giants are very bright. A blue giant is about 250,000 times brighter than the Sun. Rigel is one of the brightest blue giants. It is 10 million times brighter than the Sun.

This is a picture of the Pistol Star. It gives off more energy in six seconds than the Sun does in one year. Astronomers think it may be the most massive star ever known.

Star Clusters

Most stars in the universe are in pairs. Other stars are in larger groups of stars. The stars in these pairs and groups often circle around each other.

Usually one star in the pair or group is very bright. This is the star that is easy for people to see in the night sky. The other companion stars are dimmer. The light from the bright star blocks the light from the other stars. These dim stars are harder to see. Astronomers must look through telescopes to see these stars at all.

A binary star is a pair of two stars. Sometimes the two stars are so close that it is hard for people to tell them apart. The star pairs appear to brighten and dim in telescopes as they circle around each other. This is because the dim star passes in front of the bright star as it orbits. As it does, it blocks some of the bright star's light.

Bigger groups of stars are called clusters. Some clusters have several hundred stars. Other clusters have millions of stars. Stars in clusters are very close together. Earth's night sky would look very different if the Sun were in a crowded star cluster. The sky would be bright and full of hundreds of thousands of stars.

M80 is one of the most tightly packed star clusters in our Milky Way Galaxy. It contains hundreds of thousands of stars.

Light-Years

Astronomers use a special measurement for huge distances between objects in space. The measurement is called a light-year. This is the distance light travels in one year. A light-year equals about 6 trillion miles (9.6 trillion km). The nearest star to the Sun is Proxima Centauri. It is 25 trillion miles (40 trillion km) away. Measured in light-years, Proxima Centauri is 4.2 light-years away.

Galaxies

Galaxies are systems of stars, nebulas, and planets held together by gravity. The Sun is inside a galaxy called the Milky Way. The universe is filled with millions of galaxies like the Milky Way.

The Milky Way is a spiral galaxy. Its center is a nucleus. Some scientists believe a black hole is in the nucleus. A nuclear bulge surrounds the nucleus. The bulge is a large cluster of tightly packed old stars. Surrounding the bulge is a flat disk with large spiral arms of stars. The Milky Way looks like a giant pinwheel.

Astronomers believe the Milky Way contains more than 100 billion stars. It is about 100,000 light-years wide. The Sun is located in one of the Milky Way's spiral arms. The Sun is about halfway between the Milky Way's nucleus and the outer edge of the galaxy.

The spiral M100 Galaxy contains more than 100 billion stars. It is one of the brightest galaxies in the Virgo Cluster of galaxies.

The Pleiades Star Cluster is one of the most famous in the sky. People can see it from Earth without using telescopes. This cluster is also called the Seven Sisters.

Constellations

People in ancient times watched the sky. They saw that the stars moved in set patterns across the sky. Some stars rose in the east, moved across the sky, and set in the west. Night after night, the stars appeared in the same patterns in the sky.

People from several ancient civilizations made important discoveries about star movements. Astronomers from ancient Egypt, Sumeria, Arabia, and Chaldea tried to explain why some stars appeared to move. They found out that the stars were not moving. The turning Earth made the stars look like they were moving. The Earth spins from west to east. This makes the stars appear to move from east to west.

This modern star map shows some of the major constellations.

Star Maps

Astronomers in ancient times drew star maps. This helped them remember where and when they would see the same stars in the night sky. The astronomers divided the sky into smaller parts. They put the stars into small groups called constellations.

Astronomers mapped the first constellations 5,000 years ago. Today, scientists divide the sky into 88 constellations.

Constellation Names and Shapes

Each constellation has its own name. Astronomers wrote the names on ancient star maps. They named constellations after what the groups of stars looked like. Constellations are named after dogs, fish, bears, people, and birds. There are even make-believe creatures, such as a dragon and a half-man, half-horse centaur.

Astronomers gave constellations Latin names. In the past, Latin was the language scientists used. The constellation Canis Major is Latin for big dog. The constellation Pisces means fish. The constellation Cancer means crab. The constellation Orion is the name of a hunter in ancient stories. The constellation Taurus is a bull.

Astronomers made drawings to show how the stars of each constellation made a picture. For example, the constellation Leo forms the picture of a lion. The stars of Cygnus are inside a picture of a swan. The bull Taurus is right next to Orion in the sky. The picture of Taurus shows it charging Orion. The hunter Orion is pictured with a club to fight the bull, Taurus.

This is what the constellation Orion looks like in the sky.

Constellation Stories

Ancient peoples told stories called myths to explain why the stars were in the sky. Many of their stories were about constellations. Each constellation has a myth about how it formed.

According to myth, the constellation Aries is a ram with golden fur. People told this story about Aries. One day, two children were in trouble. Aries ran to save them. The children jumped on his back. The ram carried the children to safety. Aries was rewarded for saving the children by being made into a constellation.

The constellation Pegasus looked like a winged horse. According to a Greek story, Pegasus carried a young hero named Perseus. While over the ocean, Perseus spotted a woman in trouble. A sea monster was about to eat the woman. Perseus saved the woman and then fell in love with her. Her name was Andromeda. Pegasus, Perseus, and Andromeda were later placed in the sky.

The hunter Orion was mean to the animals he hunted. One day, a scorpion stung him. Then he saw how wrong he had been. Orion is now a constellation along with Scorpius, the scorpion.

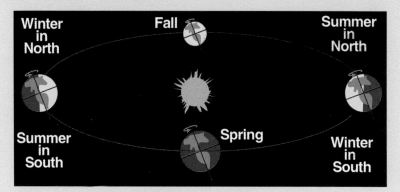

| Winter in North | Fall | Summer in North |
| Summer in South | Spring | Winter in South |

North and South

Earth is divided into two halves called hemispheres. The Northern Hemisphere and the Southern Hemisphere have opposite seasons. When the North Pole is tilted toward the Sun, the South Pole is tilted away from the Sun. This makes it summer in the north and winter in the south. When the North Pole is tilted away from the Sun, the South Pole points toward the Sun. It is then winter in the north and summer in the south.

Seasons and the Sun

Several things affect which constellations people can see at night. Observers can see different constellations depending on their locations. There are different constellations visible in the Northern Hemisphere and the Southern Hemisphere.

Also, Earth's movement around the Sun affects the appearance of constellations in the sky. Earth takes 365 days to travel around the Sun. For one part of the year, Earth is on one side of the Sun. During another part of the year, it is on the other side.

Different constellations show in the sky during different seasons. In the Northern Hemisphere in summer, the Sun's light blocks out constellations like Orion. In winter, Earth is on the other side of the Sun. People in the Northern Hemisphere can then see Orion, but the light from Scorpius is blocked.

Constellations helped ancient peoples tell what time of year it was. Each season, different constellations appear in the sky. Farmers watched for the constellations to appear in the sky. To the Egyptians, the appearance of Canis Major meant the Nile River would soon flood. When Virgo appeared in the sky, it was time to harvest the crops.

Today, people use calendars instead of stars to keep track of the seasons. But people could still use stars to track the seasons if they wanted to. Most of the constellations in our galaxy will stay like they are now for a very long time.

Glossary

astronomer (ah-STRAHN-uh-mur)—a scientist who studies objects in space

atmosphere (AT-muh-sfear)—a layer of gases that surrounds an object in space

atom (AT-uhm)—the smallest part of an element

binary (BYE-nair-ee)—two stars that are close together and orbit around each other

black hole—a region of space with so much gravity that nothing can escape it, not even light

constellation (kon-stuh-LAY-shuhn)—a group of stars that forms a pattern in the sky when seen from Earth

fusion (FYOO-shuhn)—the process where two elements combine into one; hydrogen atoms fuse together to make new helium and extra energy.

galaxy (GAL-uhk-see)—a very large system of stars, nebulas, and the objects orbiting them that are held together by gravity

nebula (NEB-yoo-lah)—a huge cloud of gas and dust in space

Internet Sites and Addresses

Astronomy Picture of the Day

http://antwrp.gsfc.nasa.gov/apod/astropix.html

Future Astronauts of America

www.faahomepage.org

**Star Child: A Learning Center for
  Young Astronomers**

http://starchild.gsfc.nasa.gov/docs/StarChild/
  StarChild.html

NASA Headquarters

Washington, DC 20546-0001

National Solar Observatory/Sacramento Peak

P.O. Box 62

Sunspot, NM 88349-0062

Space Telescope Institute

3700 San Martin Drive

Johns Hopkins University Homewood Campus

Baltimore, MD 21218

Index